Dark and Perfect Angels

BENJAMIN ALIRE SÁENZ

Dark and Perfect Angels

CINCO PUNTOS PRESS
EL PASO, TEXAS

Grateful acknowledgement is given to the following magazines in which some of these poems first appeared: *Red Dirt* ("In the Can Where She Keeps the Sugar"); *Standards* ("El Paso County Jail" and "While Sleeping At My Parents' House"); *Stanford Humanities Review* ("Arturo, Your Mother", in a slightly different version); *Sequoia* ("Contemplating Roads"); *New Letters* (the 1959 portions of "Altars into Time" appeared under the title of "The Altars of May"); *Ruah* ("Miracle in the Garden"); and *The Colorado Review* ("Uncles").

ISBN: 0-938-317-23-7
Library of Congress Number: 95-67867

FIRST EDITION

Cover photograph by Amy Dawson ©1993

Photograph of Benjamin Alire Sáenz by Cynthia Farah ©1994

NATIONAL
ENDOWMENT
FOR ❦ THE
ARTS

*This book is funded in part
by generous support from
the National Endowment for the Arts.*

Contents

Summer

Acknowledgments

WORDS are not merely material commodities in a marketplace (though, they too are bought and sold as the dollar amount on the jacket of this book will attest). Despite our preoccupations with private possessions, to work with words is to work with community property. Words are not the possession of an individual; they are not private property; they are not materials to be owned. Words arise out of the polis and must return to the polis.

I would like to acknowledge the community of workers who have labored at my side, have traded words with me, explained their meaning, their possibility, and taught me the responsibility that goes along with their use. These are citizens who have taught me my trade, and taught me, too, to embrace my limitations; these are citizens who remind that I should never take too much credit for my virtues: if there is good in me, then it is because I am the product of what is good in our culture.

Lawrence J. Schmidt, Denise Levertov, and Karen Fiser. My family (always my family): Juan and Eloisa, Linda and Mark, Ricardo and Nancy, Gloria and Anthony, Jaime, José and Sandy, John, Cynthia, Amanda, Robert, Markie, Ivana, and Ysela. And especially my wife, Patricia Macías and my step-daughter, Gabby. George Leslie Hart (who cared so much about my poems), Sara Doniach (who heard some of my work in her warm kitchen), John Tinker, Norman Campbell Robertson (Rest in peace, Norman), W.S. Di Piero, José Antonio and Cecilia Preciado Burciaga, John Ellison and Lesley Link.

I would like to express my gratitude to my teachers at the University of Louvain, the University of Texas at El Paso, the University of Iowa and Stanford University—their labor has been indispensable. They have taught me to use my mind critically, and just as importantly, they have reminded me that a mind is connected to a body, and that to disconnect the former from the latter can only lead to moral bankruptcy. The best of my teachers taught me to weigh my words carefully, to be disciplined enough to produce thoughtful work, to be sensible enough to accept that perfection is not possible, and to be intelligent enough to pay close attention to a material world which is the common site of our struggles.

A final word of thanks to the people who made this book possible: those who make the paper, those who make the ink, the printers, the designers, the proofreaders, the editors, and my publishers, Bobby and Lee Byrd. May Joseph, the worker, bless all your days. Mil gracias.

FOR
my brother, Ricardo
and for Larry.

Winter

From the city, the dying groan,
And the souls of the wounded cry for help;
Yet God pays no attention to their prayer.

—JOB 24: 12

While Sleeping In My Parents' House

Through the open window, the summer rain blew in. The cold
Wind woke me. My parents' candle blazed throughout the night—
They kept candles burning, burning, burning in their house.
I watched the flame—it fought to keep its light. Shadows
Threw themselves against the whiteness of the walls like epileptic
Sleepers whose dreams could not be loosed. (Their past
Will haunt them always. Sleep would not bring forgetting).
Though I yearned to shiver in the wind, be washed
In summer rains, I could not live with shadows in the room.
They came too close. The wind blew strong. I shut the window
Tight. My parents' flame burned bright; the curtains still;
The shadows in the room stood calm again. The light was peace.

Outside, the thunder sang a song, as if to cry against the heat
That ruled the drought. Tonight, the stars were exiled
From the skies. The lightning struck and struck; the light
Was blinking close outside the room. *Come and see, come outside
And see. I will show you all the cities of the world.* I looked
Out at the storm, and in the light could see: my father's
Rusting tools about the yard, a toy my nephew left without a thought,
My niece's skates abandoned, the piñon tree whose branches waved like
Children in distress. Then dark again—and once again the thunder.
Another flash, *Come outside and see. I will show*....Among
The things forgotten in the yard, I thought I saw myself. I was
A boy of six running toward the window of my room—and as I ran
Grew older. Closer, older still. I searched the face for signs
Of some emotion, of something he possessed that I misplaced.
The face I wore back then was lost to me. I could not hold him.
He continued running in the rain. Then everything was dark.

The thunder cried again as if to crack the desert with a whip.
And then another, louder than the last. The anger of the night
Had stilled the ceaseless howls of every fenced-in dog in every yard.
The rain was heavy, hard, pounded and pounded the house
With something more solid than rain—nails—I remembered.
I saw a boy help my father build a stronger roof. I saw
My brothers, with hammers big as their arms, pounding and nailing,
Working in a sun that scarred their skins. My father sweating
Hard, the water of his body being robbed from him. I saw
Him take a drink, moaning at the sweetness. I thought
The rain would never stop. I wondered if the roof would fall
This time. *What can a roof withstand? How long can it protect?*
It is only wood and nails. It is only melted tar. I shut my eyes
As I had shut my window. Tomorrow: nothing. What we built
Would be gone. All would be taken. I thought of the boy running
In the rain, nothing to keep him warm. I waited for quiet,
For calm. I wondered at prayers my mom and dad had uttered
As they stood before their candle in the dark. And now,
I prayed like them. I prayed like them. The sky still raging,

The sun knocking to get in, I fell asleep. When I awoke, the sun
Burned steady as the candle in the room. That light was peace.

In The Can Where She Keeps The Sugar

for my father, for his pain—
and for ours

December 1958

She works and works and works, and hums
A tune, soft and sad and slow. What blooms,
What grows inside her wordless song?
Where is her man—the handsome youth
Who watched her dance for years before
He touched her waist? Her thin fingers
Spin crooked bows wrapping the once a year
Gifts delivered this night by his father
Who never tires of caring. He entered
Softly, left quietly, careful not to wake
Her sleeping children. He hurried on, in search
Of the son she married. He knows his footsteps,
Knows where they lead, has learned to read
His tracks from other midnight hunts. He will
Return him to her door before the morning.

June 1959

He, in his thirties, tall, dark, wearing a mustache
That covers his face with night. Me, a five year old
Boy already working and working, trying to catch
His sometimes summer smile. I catch only his
Flashing eyes, bolts of lightning branding me, begging me
To bring my lips near his ear and whisper where Mom
Hid the bottle. He knows I know. I know she will

Hate me if I tell. "There!" My finger points up,
"There! In the can where she keeps the sugar."
He hugs me, reaches up, tears away the lid
Which folds like paper. He brings out the treasure
Buried in white. His fingers feel the glass
As if they were touching the smooth skin
Of a virgin. I watched his tongue lick loving
Glass like I had never seen him kiss my mother.

December 1962

Woman, you sit in your kitchen, permanent place
In life, the food you prepared all around you.
Always a harvest. The cold wind knocks. You
Do not let it enter. Where you work, it is warm.
You measure the red paper with your eyes as your hands
Tightly tape the toys. The years, hard as Aztec onyx,
Hit your face. They bruise. Your woman's work
Fences in the wind within, pushes back the tears
To the far side of your eyes where none can see them
But your God. You wait like your sleeping children.
For them, there will be food and laughter long
As you are there. Always a harvest. You sit, look
Into night, think of the lost-eyed man you married
That autumn when the cotton was ready and soft.
The picking was bad that year. Many crops have
Been planted, been plowed under since that time
Of love. The fields wait to be seeded, watered,
Wait to be touched by spring again.

Spring 1963

I ride with you on your tractor. Your neck,
Red with the slap of the sun. It is as thick as a
Trunk of a cottonwood. You shield me from the heat.
I could spend a lifetime in your shade. Like a dog
You shake your head. Your sweat rains over me,
Sprinkled in your water like at Mass. You've dropped
The bottle for the season. You rise early, plow
Your fields. You planted sugarcane this year.
We eat it raw, chew on the sweetness as solid
As the earth. The weather is good all summer.
Mama laughs as she washes. The radio on, she sings
With songs she loves. Her voice hangs
Brighter in the air than her clean laundry.

One day

You do not return from an errand into town. Mama
Watches for your truck. Drunk, you return by night.
The sweetness of the summer disappears. You are
Gone again. Lost in a world where all of us are foreign.

Spring 1964

She speaks on the phone to his mom. Outside,
It is raining. It will not be enough to end
The drought. Today, we play indoors. We watch
The anger rising in her throat competing with
The thunder: "It's the way you brought him up,
Your fault he drinks. You spoiled him, taught him
Wrong, let him roam the streets. Your fault! Now
Take him back! Let him live with you, who
Gave him life!" We echo with the damage

In her voice. She slams the phone, stomps
Into her kitchen pulling out the flour from
Its place. Her fists knead dough for daily bread.
She rolls out each tortilla flattening out her man.
The anger leaves her
                              one tortilla at a time.
She walks shyly to the phone, picks it up
And dials: "It isn't true, what I said.
You're good, so good to us. None of it was true.
I don't know why I said it." The women cry
Until their broken talk takes them on vacation.
A joke is shared, and laughter hugs the room.

Summer 1964

At dusk, the stubborn sun
Relenting, we sit
On steps and wait.   Our eyes
On country roads empty as the fields. And then
A dot appears. Nearer and nearer
Until we see a truck. Grandpa
Drives the pick-up,
Hands steady as a clock's.
The engine stops. Grandpa shoves him
From his truck, tugs him from his sleep
As if his limbs were rags.
He orders him to stand
Then knocks him down with fists. "Get up!
Your children need you."

"Gone away for help,
Your father's sick." We
Look at mama, wait for her
To smile. "No
Crying now. Back
Before you know it." "Where?"
My sister asks. "To a place
'Where he can rest." We gather
Round her voice, tie ourselves
To her. That knot is all, is life.

～

Tired of tracking you down, tired
Of searching the bars, your
Father grows old. The words he used
To touch your rotting mind
Were stronger than his fists. Did
He threaten? Did he beg? Did you
Lie there on the ground
Looking up at him who gave you life
Confusing him for God's condemning finger?
That day your father spoke
You heard his words.

～

The summer ending
You returned, no liquor on your breath. We
Watched your eyes, sad and happy as you looked
Lost to us. My younger brothers hung about
Your arms as though you were an oak. I held back
My touch. I buried deep my joy
Same as I did the tears. Is he healed?
Will he get lost again?

July 1990

A visit to his house,
That man who always searched
Until he found my father.
That man with wadded skin.
That tired man whom God
Is pressing with his palms. The lone
Survivor, his peers
No longer walk above the ground.
His front door
Open, but he is not inside.
I find him in the yard, looking
Toward the roof. "The air conditioner's
Broken. Too old for climbing
Ladders. Your dad will
Have to fix it." He walks inside
Weaving as though drunk. *Get up!*
Your children need you! His crooked
Hands can't tighten into fists. His legs
Are straw, his back
Is now a bow. There is no future
In his eyes. But there, the past
Is clear.
                    I sit beside
The man who gave me dimes,
Who taught me to take worn shoes
And shine them back
To life. *"Mis hijos, Benny.*
Me dieron tanta lata...."

His lips spit out a memory
Of how my father's workers
Never worked a lick, of how they sat
Shaded under trees
As my father drank his days
Or how he couldn't pay
For tractors that he bought.
Grandpa, don't. Don't take me
To that farm. We've moved away.

August 1990

You've stayed
Sober.   Twenty-six years.
What was it like, those years of
Drink and exile? Was that place good
Where you went to cleanse your body
And your heart? Did you shake for weeks?
Repentant, did your back bend
Beneath the heavy penance
That the God of thirst demanded?
Did you sleep? Did you dream of us
Who waited? Did you ever park the truck
Outside a bar, and tremble in the seat?
How many times did someone offer you
A beer? How many times did you think
Of letting it flow
Through your blood *one more time, just*
One more time? Does it turn
And turn and turn inside your head

Or are those days so dark
That to think of them at all
Is to fall into a grave
With no hope of an ascension?

～

You did not break
Beneath those years of thirst,
But, Dad, those awful years
Were never yours alone. They did not
Break that stubborn girl
Who used to dance with others
Before she danced with you.
They did not break
Your father
As faithful as your wife.
Your sons and daughters
Do not hide in shadows. We live
Most days in light. Like the desert
We were born in, we need
No rain to bloom.
But there are nights
When winds kick up the dirt
And blow the memories back. They beat
Stomping through my house
Louder than my heart.
A boy, unchanged by time,
Pulls me toward a kitchen:
"There! There! In the can
Where she keeps the sugar!"
And when he leaves
I am drunk remembering.

El Paso County Jail

In the holding tank
an old man,
life stealing
all his teeth,
talks of a finer
past. Life
has not yet
robbed him
of his speech.

"Used to walk the streets,
beer in one hand, 'nother in my pocket,
talk and laugh and strut,
girls all over me,
and cops didn't give
no rat's ass. Used to be
they knew my name, even took me
home from time to time. Never
had no car. Streets
back then were full.
Only time I got hauled in
was when I let off steam
and belted punks
who needed beltin'.
Now, I get hauled in
just for walkin' 'round drunk.
Cops ain't civilized
no more."

⮜

Such a sunny day, spring biting me everywhere. Just
had to take a spin, feel the road, the air, and
then, standing there, my legs spread, hands
behind my back, handcuffed, hands all over me.

⌒

And a man, face

scarred like

tires ran over

his face

and left

their treads forever.

Born in Shreveport,

Tells me

jails aren't so bad

"It's them prisons, boy, a kind
of shit-hole hell. You don't
know nothin' 'bout that, boy.
Mexican, ain't you? Been in
with you people before, Know
some words: *puta, pendejo,
cabrón.* Yeah, I know some
words. Like to say *fuck* though, *fuck,*
it's a good word. Ya know,
a psych-i-ti-tris told me once
I was schizophrenic. And I says
to him: 'Good,
let the other guy pay.'"

⌒

Through the window

in the steel

door, we

listen, watch

others

move about.

Ten of us

in this room,

no cigarettes

allowed. Not here.

We wait

some of us to

be let out

once we make

a call,

and some will just

move on

to a room

with fewer

cellmates, but

where they let

you smoke.

❧

In handcuffs   on the sidewalk.
People stare.
Chicano cop eyes me,

watches how my head bows
till it's almost on the ground,
keeps me on display
for twenty minutes.

❧

He shakes and shakes his head. No wrinkles
yet, a kid. He looks up, then down again.
Rises from his seat, paces back and forth,
back and forth. "So," he looks at me,
"What did you do to get—I mean, like,
what did you do?"

"Traffic ticket. They say I didn't pay a
fine. I say I paid. Computer says I didn't."

Across the room, a man with tattoos large
as his arms nods his head and laughs. He looks
like my younger brother, long hair, eyes afraid
of nothing. "Don't screw with no computers, man.
Gringo computers got big dicks—fuck us all."

"A goddamned ticket?" Shreveport laughs,
"Hell, that ain't nothin'."

"Me, too," the kid smiles. "Only I have
more than one. See, I got four tickets,
and, like, I never told my parents. Next week
I'll be graduating. Just forgot. Like, I don't
think my old man's gonna like this scene."
He shakes his head again.

❧

In there
I remembered
how I'd often sat
and watched
the dark people
standing outside
the gray jail
on San Antonio Street,
women and boys
looking up
every day
at the building
prayers on their lips
as if they were standing
at the graves
of their dead
waiting for them
to rise.

❧

"Broke parole," he says. "That
son of a bitch hit me
with a pool stick. What
the fuck was I supposed to do?
My wife gots two kids.
Be another year
before I'm out again. Won't
see 'em for a while. Guess

she'll have to move in
with my mom again. I'm gettin'
like my old man. Never
saw him much, spent lots of time
in dumps like this. Mom never
said nothin', just
did a lot of waitin'."

⌒

The seconds here
are loud. A man
dark   in a corner
looks out
what passes for
a window.
I catch
his glare,
eyes that bite
like starving teeth.
The words are clear
in him: I could kill
you. Anyone.
This goddamn city.

"I Wouldn't Even Bleed"

He appeared, white as any angel:
"¿Me regalas un cigarro?" Not his
native tongue.
      I handed him the pack:
"All yours."
      He grabbed at them
and stuck one in his mouth.
"English is good. You don't look
American."
      "Tell me what one
looks like."
      He smiled, "You want
we should grab a beer?" Nothing
of a beggar in his voice, nothing
of a boy.
      "Don't know you," I
turned to walk away.
      He grabbed
my arm: "Just got out," he said
pointing at the Juárez jail's wall.

      "How long
you been in there?"
      "A couple
years, or maybe three. Doing time
is doing time
not counting it."
      "How'd you
get yourself in jail?"

"I took the rap—"
he stopped himself,
        "Don't want to talk 'bout that.
I burned that bridge."
        "Where you from?"
        "Texas."
        "Big state," I said.
        "Yeah, big state," he said, "you wanna
grab a beer?"
        "Look," I said, "You need
some cash?"
        "No money, man, just
buy my beer."

        We drank—not much, ate
food. He swallowed fast, then asked
for mine. He was hungry still
after plates were licked. He talked,
his words like steps in an old abandoned house.
He spoke about a girl who'd made him feel
as though he might stop breathing, as though
his heart would stop at any minute.
"What I did, I did for her." The table
shook beneath his pounding fist.
Even in the light his eyes were dull.
I thought they'd once been blue
but something faded them
like a book left out—forgotten—
in the unforgiving sun of Texas summers.

I drove across the border, and when
the *migra* asked where we were born,
it took a while before he said "American."
He looked so white and Texan, they
let us come across.

"You're home," I said.

       "Texas," he said as he spit,
"ain't nothin' but a grave." He looked at me,
then laughed. "You got a knife?"
I shook my head. "Too bad." He laughed
and laughed. "If you cut me up,
I wouldn't even bleed."

Meditation: Winter

Now from the sixth hour there was darkness over all the land until the ninth hour. And about the ninth hour Jesus cried with a loud voice, "Eli, Eli, lama sabach-thani?" that is "My God, my God, why hast thou forsaken me?" And some of the bystanders hearing it said, "This man is calling Elijah....Let us see whether Elijah will come to save him."

—Matthew 27: 45-49

Despedida I
December 30, 1991

"You look
like a college boy."

He spoke to me
soft—a child.

He is tired, he is
lost. Simple,

Simple now
in speech—

a new innocence
powerless

to stop the ninth
hour. Soon

the darkness will
come. Silence

Will swallow his
heart. The last

drought will turn
his blood to

sand; the wind
will scatter

the grains. We will
search the earth

but find no trace
of his remains. Nothing

can save his body,
but he will not

die without finding
a voice to speak

again—letting it
float in the

world just one more
one more time:

Up! Up! Let it go,
let it fly! Up!

Up! Eli Eli Elijah,
do you see?

I have come
unwillingly to this

unholy town
to witness this event.

I come to do
what God requires

of me, his strange
voice singing

singing in my ear:
You must you must.

I have traveled
a long distance

in the worst time
of the year,

*the weather sharp, the very
dead of winter.*

I confess it: I
suffered little

on my journey—
had no hard

time of it. No
cold coming

(a painless trip:
a plane has

eased the crossing
of many deserts).

The earth and sky
were absent—

yet I saw all
the flashing, colored

lights of the dirty
hostile cities

of the world.
I followed

no star. I come
bearing no

gifts—this child,
Norman, has no need

of them. I do not
come to worship

or kneel before
a Christ.

This is a child.
This is a child.
This is the very
dead of winter.

Despedida II
December 31, 1991 / January 1, 1992

I refuse to describe—him—refuse
To paint the thief that steals his breath.
A terrible beauty is....The words spill
Out. I repeat, repeat the words, then
Shake them off. *Yeats, I want you out!*
I exorcise your presence from this room.
This is not your place. I will not
Make this good. How could this be beauty?

"Benjamin,
Do you still have that penthouse in New York?"
"Norman, no, I never had a penthouse. I'm still

In school." "Hummm. Where am I?" "Norman,
At St. Joseph's in Chicago." "Oh, I have
To catch a flight." "No, you have to get
Some rest. Your job's to rest." He no longer
Knows his own address: I give him the street
And the number. He disagrees, does not remember
Living there. He is certain only of his
Flesh because he feels its pain. He is
Leaving his memory behind, but the fact
Of the body remains. "Benjamin, help me
Dress. I have to catch a flight." "Norman,
Rest. We've missed the flight—it's New Year's Eve.
It's cold." "New Year's Eve? And are you
Going out?" "No, I thought I'd stay
With you." "It doesn't sound like fun."

                    He falls asleep.
I watch him breathe. I shut the book I hold.
I used to love these words. I don't want them
now. My faith in books is leaving me tonight.
How will I live? What will I think of the words
When the words belong to me? Are they mine?
They are Yeats', they are Wordsworth's,
They are Pound's, they are Lorca's. They are
William Carlos Williams'. They were
Never mine.
                A nurse steps in,
And smiles. I look at her. She whispers
"Happy New Year." I repeat her words
And give them back to her. Happy? And new?
Norman, what's a year?

Despedida III
January 5, 1992

Why do you stay alive?
I watch myself sitting next
To him. I watch his sisters
And his mother care for him.
I see his father searching
The floor in grief as if
He expects to find a cure
Somewhere in the places
Where he's stepped. I see
His lover's face: distant,
Full of loss, empty, a dry
River that will miss
Its water forever. So much
Hurt, yet no one here is breaking.
But it is not we who are dying. We
Will come and go, and speak of politics
And art, speak of wars between
The races and the sexes. We will
Come and go and speak of God
And peace. But the subject here
Is death. We will walk out
The door. If we look back,
Then we will damn him to the deepest
Regions of Hell—or perhaps

Be turned to a pillar
Of salt or stone or shit. *Blessed
Are those who don't look back.*
I will not look back. I will be
Blessed forever. I watch him as
He lies on the bed that has
Become a part of him. I will
Not remember him—not
This way. When I remember
Him, I will remember his youth.
He will be strong in my memory—
I can work miracles there. I will
Succeed in erasing his physical
Death. I sit next to him, take
His hand. He is no longer close
To me. But there is still this
Face, and I know that I still
Know it. If I cling to his hand,
Then maybe I can keep the
Rhythms in his speech from
Flowing out of him, maybe I can
Keep—*Rise. In the name
Of the Lord of Hosts, I command you
To*—If I hold on
To his hand, then I can hold
The memory of a man, healthy
And full of a sun and a sea,

And a wind that cleans the sky.
If I hold on, maybe I'll remember
That he was   *Adíos. Me despido*
De tu alma, de tu corazón,
Me despido de tu cuerpo.

Interlude
January 5, 1992

He smiled through thick
glasses   *God, it's good*
to see   Larry
at the Minneapolis airport.
His familiar face—like
being home again. But who am I
to him? An apparition
from his past. What exactly does
he see? *You look like a college*
boy. Norman, I'm pushing forty.
College-boy days are over.
Norman, before your eyes go
blind   tell me what you saw.

⤙

        Four hours in an airport,
So we talked. And talked. His wife,
his job, my going back to the desert, to the border,
you'll be happy there. Listen,
listen, it's not the words

that always matter; it isn't what

we see. No one sees exactly.

Listen, it's the voice. Larry, let me

hear you talk. There are times when

some of us are perfect, when our joy

is so complete, when everything

converges, and the green

in our speech is tender and soft:

spring leaf *mirroring* the goodness

of the earth. He sits across from me—

I see that he is perfect. Perfect's

the material word for holy. Larry, talk me

into living. Talk me, tell me,

yell: the winter will not kill

you   me   everything.

Hypothermia I
January 10, 1992

"The doctor says he's lasted long
Because his heart was strong, because
His heart was young. And now it's come
To this…" I could sense the numbness
In his voice. The sadness, too.
"Hypothermia," he said. I asked him
What it meant. "His body's lost its heat.
His hands and feet are cold." A month ago
His skin and voice were warm. His lover kept

A certain calm, refused to kiss that nothingness
Reaching for his face. I held the phone,
Just sat, just listened to his voice.

About a week now since I left him
In Chicago as he slept. From his quiet
Private room, you could see the Lake, but
It was gray and dark—a mirror for this city
In December. *"What city am I in?"* *"Chicago,*
Norm, remember?" *"Yes, yes, is this my bed?*
Help me to the bed—I need to rest."

I kissed his forehead—bye—*you have been*
So loved, and it is all that matters. Love
Is all that matters? If I believed that lie,
Then I could sleep tonight. I want
Tonight to enter sleep's forgetting.

Hypothermia II
January 11, 1992

Were you led all this way for death? For death alone. I thought your final
words to me would be, well, I was going to keep them, repeat them,
remember them always until it was a song, a song, a song. When I got
back to California it was raining. Water is good for the earth, but I did
not rejoice. I wanted sun. But today—today was sunny. David just called
and said you were dead. He sounded tired, and he whispered your name
as if he were uttering the name of a saint. Now I know why my grand-
mother whispered the names of the dead. I looked up at the calendar and
made a mental note of the date: I don't remember your birthday, but I will
remember the day of your death. Tomorrow is *Holy Name Sunday*. Your

funeral Mass will be on Thursday. The dead will not bury the dead—it is the task of the living. I will stay in California and light a candle on my altar. Wendy is sending me your picture—the one where you look happy and young, the one where you're dressed in a tux and holding your violin. I have a tape of you playing in a concert. Sometimes I clap with the audience. Joellen and I cleaned out the garage today. It seems like a relief. You were so sick at the end. It's cold outside, but not as cold as Chicago. Hannah's been sick—Karen had to take her to the vet. I told David to get some rest. I told him I'd visit him. I really will, Norman, I'll visit him— but not in the winter. In the winter, Chicago has hypothermia. Cold gray winter days will always remind me. Karen's going to have an operation on her birthday. We knew this day would come. You didn't think it would come this soon. What's it like not to need a body? Did I ever tell you that I didn't like California? When I visited you in the hospital you asked me: "Are you visiting relatives in Chicago, Benjamin?" "No," I said, "you're my only relative in Chicago." My answer confused you. In the chapel of St. Joseph's hospital, one of the stained glass windows shows St. Vincent de Paul healing the sick. They say he could work miracles. Miracles, Norman, they have become so common we don't even call them that anymore. Your first breath: that was a miracle. So was your last. Norman, the dead, do they love? Benjamin, do the living?

Los Vivos Piensan de los Muertos.
Tuesday, January 14, 1992

The living mourn the dead, but
Secretly rejoice. The Angel
Of Death has made his choice.
Touch. Feel our flesh. It is
Warm as a day embraced by
Morning light. Today, we are safe.

We wake, the sun is there,
We make coffee, read and
Curse the headlines, brush our
Teeth, make plans to go
To dinner with old lovers,
With old friends. There's never
Enough time—we do what
We can. It's not a bad
Life—promising career,
Loyal friends—could be worse,
Could be better. What if
It were taken? What if
Someone took it? Not
If you're careful. Careful—
That's the key. The homeless
Lived reckless, gambled and
Lost. We read the obituary pages
Looking for people
We know. Ah, but he was old.
Poor sucker. Well, he's dead.
Maybe he deserved it—
Smoked too much, drank too hard,
Ate fried foods and red meat.
But he lived a good life.
They're lesser beings, the dead.
We, who work, who've lived
Right lives, have the strength
To walk out the door—see, smell
The flowers we planted
In Spring—see, beautiful.

Oración
Thursday, January 16, 1992

Today, Karen had surgery. She made herself
Brave. Always there's the chance that —

She's come through. In her room
At the contagious hospital, she made a joke,

"My dignity." She winced—again the pain.
The light, dull as her voice. Balloons floated

over her body, her bed. *Happy Birth*—I wanted to—
I was very—*Up! Up! Let it go, let it fly*   I felt

teeth—gnawing at my heart. I had tried
So hard to put down the rebellion of this

Hurt. *Happy New*   And there I was—that room
Almost in tears—there is work to do. I am trying

To be calm. I am trying to be grateful for
My life. I am trying hard to praise the great

Creator—but I hear Job's wife *Curse God, Ben,
And die. God? God is a set of jaws that*

Bites down on your heart. Two years since
My niece was killed. Almost two years since

I felt my sister sobbing in my arms. *They hurt,
They hurt my Amy. I want her back. Ben,*

I want her back. Did I just leave Chicago?
Was I ever there? Norman, do you believe

In words? This afternoon I went
To Mass. No one knew—him—knew

Today a Mass was being held—for him—
In a Chi Town church. I lit a candle

for Karen, and another for the repose of the soul
of Norman Campbell Robertson. *Give to me*

Your perfect. Let me hear you talk. Larry,
Talk me back to living. Night, the sun is

Down. The house is empty. The candle burning
On my altar does not warm my room. It's cold,

It's cold in here. At night it's hard.
I don't believe in light—that it ever

Was, that it will come again. The world
Has sinned—the sun is gone. Life

Will always be like night. Dark and nothing,
Nothing, yet I hear: *"Elijah, ven y sálvanos."*

Is that my voice? It's cold. *Elijah, come.*
Come and save us all.

In Memoriam:
Norman Campbell Robertson

Novena for
a Lost Ancestor

I see his eyes, awful even now.
I see his thick stern lips, the hint of a smile
he never wore in life.

I.

The Romance of Ventura's Father

Thou met'st with things dying,
I with things new born.
        —A SHEPHERD, THE WINTER'S TALE

Autumn 1893
Europe

Still, in the dusk, autumn pressed against him,
Heavy like the air, like his heart. He fell old
Into his usual sleep, exhausted from his life.

                Next morning he woke, his sweat
Pouring out a smell as if he had swallowed a rare bird,
Caged it within his ribs—and still the bird flew inside,
Its wings beating out a freedom. Drunk in the aroma,
He remembered, years since he thought of it
(Years since he thought of his lungs and his chest
And his hair, years since he thought of the air
And the earth that was killing). *Young, I am young.*
He had forgotten.

           That same afternoon, the harvest just begun,
He took a torch, flung it through the sky as if to rip it,
And lit his waiting wheat (a good year, too, and long
Awaited after countless years of drought. The summer's
Generous rain was everything he'd prayed for).
His season's work in flames, he clapped his hands, tapped
His foot to the tune of the burning song. His whistling
Could be heard among the fires, incense rising white
Above black smoke. *I should have made this music long ago.*

The night before,
Corn had come to him in sleep, the leaves swaying
To the beat of his breath, the tassels tossing him bits
Of bread untasted. He had never imagined such grace,
Never seen such green. The life in his crops, pale
And tired, and not even now, in their dying,
Dressed in flames, could they equal the dance
Of the strange stalks in his dream.

New Year's Eve 1893
Mexico City.

In the plaza, the midnight clock struck
Loud. The bells, as if oblivious to winter, rang out
Twelve times. The expectant crowd embraced, arms swimming
Strong in a sea of abrazos. Their Spanish, drowning out
The bells, covered the cold with shouts that hung like blankets
In the night. *¡Año nuevo! ¡Año nuevo!* The peónes'
Muscled arms waved light as flags, veins thick as women's
Braids running warm with drink, running quick with blood
That kept close the memory of a hundred revolutions
Nailing anger to their bones. *¡Año nuevo! ¡Año nuevo!*
Limpios en las aguas del año inocente, siempre inocente.

Here, in this Mexico, is where he found himself.
Here among the peasants who touched so easily, whose
Joyous shouts rang out as if they came from angels who had
Bartered with their God, tossing back their wings
For the right to work their land. Warm in these strange
Waters, he swam among the brown. He could have drowned
In those faces. *Will they mix with me? I, with my skin*
That clashes with their songs? Will they mix with me?

Autumn 1894
Sierra Tarahumara

"Tus ojos tan verdes," she said the day she met him,
Peasant Indian of the fields. And though her words
Were soft as they were clear, she spoke beyond his reach.
He thought the sad lack of sun in his skin would make
Her sick. He turned to go—she caught his hand in hers.
She touched the leaves of corn, greener in her shadow
Than in light—and then she pointed at his eyes as if to say:
Your eyes are green as leaves. He could have stood
Forever in her shade.

                From her, he learned
About the mysteries of the corn, grew strong on her harvest.
She blew into his mouth her gift of words until the language
Of his birth had disappeared. After the first freeze,
They clung to each other's limbs like leaves refusing
To fall, neither one aware when winter came and left.
When autumn came again, it was he who picked the corn.
She watched and rested. She waited patient, large
As a yellow moon from their season of touch.

             Before winter came again,
He held his son in Indian summer arms. As dark as she,
Their child: fruit of the new world no longer carrying
The weight of his pallid skin. Together, they named him
Ventura. The name means luck, a tale of good fortune.
Ventura, it means to gamble, to risk all—everything.

II.

The Unchronicled Death of Your Holy Father

For the record: there is no record
of your father's death. He died
of a disease that is today

                          preventable.

In the land where you were
born, the current century has not
arrived—not so much as one damn gangrene
foot in the goddamn door—and so

> *If your old man were alive today,*
> *He'd live the same. He'd die the same.*

Since there is no record, I have elected
myself as chronicler. I have inherited
the unhappy task of representing
your father's death. It falls to me
to pick a name for your disease—
we cannot live in the country
of vague generalities. (In my chosen vocation,
lying is permissible—encouraged—
but the lies must be specific).
Cholera perhaps? Yes,

> *Cholera will do—it's in the news again.*
> *A common fate? Why not? He was a common man.*

As you well know, I know little
of your father, since you never spoke

to me—except to shout. Grandchildren
were not your forte. My natural inclination
is to write about our failed friendship
But this is about you—so let me
sympathetically continue:

You loved him, your father, loved him
to the point of obsession. You loved
the way he struggled with his Spanish,
spoke it like a child because he came
from a place
                          of another language.
You saw his country in his green eyes
and hated *hated* your mother. The villagers
told you he married beneath his station. It was
not his fault. That dark Indian orphan
bewitched him with powder and herbs.
It was clear his love was unnatural.
It was common knowledge
she came from a family of witches:

> *The color of his skin won great respect*
> *But where your mother walked, the people spit.*

You watched him grow weaker. Your mother stood by
and did nothing. Where were her
herbs and powder? She could have saved him.
You watched him taking his last
breath, and still she refused
to work her magic. All she did was pray
before a worthless cross. She saw you sad,
and tried to comfort you:

"Have faith, have faith, the saints won't let him die."
He died. Inside you screamed: "She lied! She lied!"

When she wept over his cold corpse,
you refused to believe in her tears.
Can it be that witches cry? You
walked away from her:

"Stupid Indian woman, you told me he would live."

Her grief was hers. Your grief was
yours. Separate in your sorrow, you ran
to that river where
he taught you to swim and fish.
There you slammed your dark
body against the stones and howled
like a wolf in a trap: *Why*
did he die? Why did he live?
Me? Is that his great gift
to the world? Me? You looked
at your reflection in the water
of the river that you loved. You saw
your mother—Indian and dark—nothing
of your father in your face—and after a night
of howls, you locked his image
in your heart and never again
let him out. And so, I your grandson,

Who never learned your father's name,
Sit here writing of your boyhood pain.

III.
The Girl You Left Behind

Buried him deep, you and she. No priest
to rub the oils on his skin.
No sacraments, no prayers from the book,
no sacred songs to fling him into heaven.

The shovel, heavy as you dug—you
and she—heavy as the grief your black eyes
kept. Without a word, you pierced
the waiting ground. You dug, taking
turns, her
              then you then her again
not touching
                when you passed
that tool between you. You shared
his love—now you shared this work.
                    Deeper and deeper
you dug, you and she: the hole where you'd
place your treasure. Now, he would sleep
alone—not with her. Never again
with her. He would wake to virgins
and to angels. He would not
wake to her. He would not wake to you.

⌒

1991. The Streets of Juárez:
Tarahumaran Women

They sit, ubiquitous, more numerous than mangos at the market.
These women raise their children on the street—raise them

To the dawn from their ungiving beds (cement is hard, but it is free).
They wake dark sons, then stare at wanting eyes. Alive, today

Alive: the raising of the dead, their morning rites. No ahhhs
For common miracles. If their faith can work such wonders, then

Let them raise hell and revolution: We must have jobs! We must
Have jobs! But look, they lack the strength to raise their hands

Let alone their fists and voices: their bodies cupped like leaves—
Shriveled—begging for water from the sky. Any coin will do. But

When a nickel hits their palms, they pretend they've lost their sight.
They pretend they cannot feel the cold hard drops of rain. They do not

Praise the god that stops to drop spare change in their
Unworthy hands. (Are there no jobs? Are there no jobs?) They give

Nothing in return. They will not explain their lives. They are
There. They sit. Filth and flies. What sort of mothers raise

Their children on the street? A dollar buys no nod. Their faces hide their
Hearts, their shame (if it is shame), their pain (there must be pain).

They will not speak. A dollar buys no comfort, buys no home;
It buys no love. But a dollar does buy bread. Where is gracias

For the bread?
            It's not that gratitude and gracias can't
Be bought, but it will cost a little more than these small

Drops—it will not end the drought. On holy days, the women
Flash their teeth: their lightning cuts the sky.

They give the pissing gods the homage they demand.
They celebrate and praise for reasons of their own.

Out of respect for the dead
but no respect for your mother who was
living
      a few men
from the village laid him in the hole
that you and she had dug. When they began
covering him with dirt
                      she banished them. Alone
she began to blanket him with earth.
You watched unable to help.
She flung off her rebozo, sweat
pouring from the darkness of her skin
but you felt nothing
not for her. *She did not save him. She*
did not save him: it is all you kept
repeating. When her widow's work was done,
her husband covered with the winter of the earth,
she knelt and wept. You watched, waited,
you wanted her to break, but she did not.
Instead of pounding her breasts,
Instead of hurling curses at her God
and crumbling in her hurt,
she took her trembling finger and pressed it
in the dirt: wrote her husband's name
and walked away.

She looked back,
and beckoned: *Ventura.* You
shook your head. Again she called your name.
Again you shook your head. "How will I live?"
she begged. Shaking and shaking your head—
you would not stop. You closed your eyes.
"How will I live?" You turned
from her.

        You rubbed away her writing from
his grave, erased the traces of her finger
from the earth.

        You stood outside her shack,
the place of your conception and your birth.
You uttered parting curses at her who gave you life:
"You will know no peace. You, who let him
die, will know no peace."

IV.

Going North

You listened to the lore,
legends of a country
farther north. You knelt
before the men who told
the tales
          and you believed:
"Glory in that kingdom; cities,
cars, money; people there
have doctors—they don't die;
women, whiter than your father;
and every man's a god."
Yes, you believed, and then
prepared to leave.

                    Walking
past your green-eyed father's grave,
you grabbed a fist of dirt
and stuffed it, angry,
in the pocket of your coat—
the only piece of earth you'd ever love.

          Which road?
Which road went north?
Which way to the land
where she could never find you—

her and her skin
and her ways? Which path to that
country of doctors and
no death?

        Walk north, walk
north, walk north to
the land of forgetting.

V.

Chihuahua: City of the Lost

You turn your face
From the village of your birth—holy
To your mother and those who came before.
What are trees and rivers? What are birds
To you?—they fly but are not free.
That village full of makers? Baskets and pots
And carvings of angels and saints.
They lull themselves to sleep with
Prayers as old as God. What is
Soil? It gives only beans and corn.
Beans and corn—no art, no magic
In farming. What is sky—blue—
Bluer than Spaniards' eyes? *Sierra Tarahumara,*
Who hears your name except the wind?
You turn away. Sacred? Not to you.

Five days, you walk
A hunger written on your body (You'd drink
A lifetime after this—and still
You'd want). Where you going, boy? Where you going?
Walking toward the desert? This? This? This
In exchange for your mountains?

Reaching a house
On a dirty lonely road, you swallow tears
And pride, and beg for food. "Where you going, boy?"
The woman asks. "North," you say. The ragged lady
Of the house feeds you beans and corn, tells you that

El Norte is a devil. "Don't go," she warns, "don't
Tempt the hand of God. Dollars for your soul—you want
Dollars, boy?" You nod your head. "How old are you?"
"Eighteen." She laughs. She knows about sons
And their ways, and how their lies begin. "Look," she says,
"You have to work—save money for your journey
To the north. In Chihuahua you can work. It's a city
For the broken and the lost. No one cares that you live
Except for God, and He won't say a word.
My oldest son will take you to that place."

                            ❧

                        Arriving in Chihuahua
The woman's son takes you to a bar. He buys you
Your first drink. He speaks with a man whose voice
Is heavy as the fat around his waist. He points to you,
Then calls you to the table where they sit. Brother
To the woman whom you met, who fed you beans and corn.
"You'll work for me," he says. He gives you work
That pays you next to nothing. At least you have a place
Where you can sleep. At least he gives you food.
Five years you work. You watch, and speak
When spoken to. The people have no land. They own
The streets. You learn their ways. You perfect
The art of rolling cigarettes, each one singular
And sweet—you smoke them with love. You become
Enamored with the not-so-subtle joys of being drunk—
All those words you keep locked in your head: safe
And swimming—trying to hang on to life. The words
Drown before they reach your lips.

One evening in an alley
You have your first woman, or better, she has you.
She clamps you between herself
                          until she makes you shake,
Until you fall. You are graceless in her arms. And when
You moan, she spits, then walks away. "No good," she says,
"I've had much better men."

Indians sleep in shacks. They work
But have no homes. They look like people of your village,
Look like you   like you   as if you leapt to life
From a common Indian womb. But you pretend you do not
Know their language or their ways. When you get drunk
You spit on them—and want to beat them into dust.
You see the rich ride horses—you stand outside their homes.
You curse them as you lie awake at night. You want to see them
Homeless; you want to see them bleed. You see cantinas
Filled with men who drink too much and hate too much—
Who drop the anger of their lives on the bodies
Of the women that they fuck, but cannot love. You see
Churches filled with women, and with candles, and with children,
And with hope. Milagros covering the feet of every statue;
Some are silver, some are tin: heads and hearts, arms and legs.
They reflect the light of burning wicks, of women's prayers;
they are whispers in the silence of Chihuahua.
You see people crawling to the altar on their knees.
A bottle in your hand, you stand outside and laugh.

There is nothing in this city that you love. Alone
There are tears, but you hide them from yourself.

You repeat the words the woman spoke to you: city
Of the broken   and the lost.

     No one   will care if you live.

       One night, with your guitar, you sit
And sing. You do not hear the sorrow in your voice
Nor do you hear its goodness. You walk into the night.
You do not stop until you reach the border. You swim across
The river. "I am free," you yell. "A new man. I am free."

VI.
Braided Woman

The ripe green fields of chile, ready
For summer picking. She knelt on the banks of the ditch
The water muddy and red; the sky so hot it was white;
Your lips so lonely they were trembling. She was scrubbing
Clothes on a board, lifting the dirt from the shirts
With the power of her hands

cleansing the sins of her children.
Their shirts would be whiter than snow. She was born to make things
Soft. She sang a song you heard on Chihuahua's busy streets.

Hay unos ojos que si me miran
Hacen que mi alma tiemble de amor

Her voice, calm as the desert sand on a breezeless day in spring.
I could walk on her desert forever. This was the land that was
Promised. Her eyes erased the path of the return. *Mexico is dead,*
my mother's face forgotten. You opened your palm as if
To catch her voice, but her song was not

for you. That morning,
Standing there, you did not want to breathe, afraid that any movement
Would make her disappear. *Eternally walk in my sight.* Her braids
Wrapped her head, thick and dark (so black they were almost green)
Like vines embracing a tree.

Wrap around me. Wrap around me.

That summer day, you
Followed her, watched her

Embrace her sons, three of them
Waiting for her return. Where
Was their father? Where was
This angel's husband? You asked
The men of the village. Dead,
They said. She had two. The first
Was killed by a train, the second drowned
In the river. No one
Wants her now. Her beauty
No good, a curse. Men
Move away from her. She was good
For God, the only man
She would not outlive.

Under the crescent moon, you asked to know
Her name, and then her secrets. She smiled, then
Said shyly: *Teresa, like the little flower of Jesus.*
Then she told you how she'd dreamed her husbands'

Deaths:

> *Javier was the first.*
> *I was just a girl. When I*
> *was with him, my heart became*
> *a hand that ached to touch*
> *his face. I think the angels*
> *prayed to have skin*
> *as smooth, as dark as his.*

At sixteen we were married. At eighteen
he was dead. God sent me his death in a dream,
a gift that's mine forever. He was traveling
on a horse. The sun had set, the great darkness
coming. In my dream the stars were falling
to the ground. The train was near.
Startled by the noise of the machine,
the horse tossed him on the track.
"Javier!" I yelled, "Get up!"

I was widowed for a year, and then
Andrés (who'd chased me all his life)
begged to marry me. I preferred
the dead—such perfect lovers—than to marry
men of flesh.
                    To love once is holy,
but twice, a sin. God would punish
such greed.

"I will give you children!"

He spoke the magic words.
Javier had left me with a womb
hungry for children.

Three sons, he gave me, my Andrés, then promptly
drowned. The river is the hungriest of wombs.
God sent his death in a dream.
Another gift.
                    No daughters. I am still starving
for daughters."

You were more hungry for her
Than she for little girls.
You placed your hand on her cheek:
"I will give you many, many daughters."

And so you did   Five of them   And added two more sons.
   You undid   Her braids   And loved her
   And then   Left her   For the bottle.

VII.

Lullaby for Your Family

Hush my babies, go to sleep
I know your eyes are sad
But Mama's here, she'll keep you warm:
Sleep safe, sleep calm, sleep deep.

She's had enough of children but not enough of food.
Her husband wants another, and yells that God wants
More. She fights his grip, and yells she'll have another
When Angels gift her with a vision in a dream.

They sleep in separate rooms, and rest alone. She has
Banished him. Each to the bed of their making: She
With novenas and saints; he with his bottle of rum. Each
To their separate comforts, each to their separate dreams.

Go to sleep, now all of you
Your dad is drunk and gone.
But he'll be back soon—sober
Don't count the days, they're long.

He's gone a night, he's gone a week, he's gone
A month. He's unpredictable. "Your fault I leave," he tells
His wife. "You've turned my children from me with your talk
Of God and prayers. Like my mother, you're a witch."

He slams the door. When he returns, he's thin and needs
A bath. At times when he comes back, he sobs with grief.

More often he is angry and curses all his children and his
Wife. His daughters care and feed him back to life.

> *Go to sleep, and be at peace,*
> *Forget life's troubling cares*
> *And in your dreams the kisses*
> *Of your father will not cease.*

VIII.

Confessions of Benjamín, Your Grandson

A year ago, in anger,

you flew inside my

house. (I left a window

open by mistake.)

You nested in my head.

I wrote some words

to make you fly away:

~

Ventura's Visits

He made adobes in his youth though
When I met him all he did was sit. He liked to pose
For pictures, chin up, chest out, back straight and
Stiff. I was banished, unworthy of his time
Though time is all he had. He spent it on himself.

At six, I ran from him, ran from the smell
Of his well-starched khaki shirts. (The immaculate
Clothes he wore like armor could not protect him
From the smell of forty years of drink.) At seven,
I wanted to crush his bones to dust as he chased me
Away with "Chivo! Chivo!" and a fist clenched so tight
That Guadalupe herself could not have calmed it open.

I was in high school when he died. My youngest brother
Wept. My mother, reared in the ways of loss, grieved

Respectfully. For me, his death meant a holiday
From school. I only visited his grave because
They laid him next to his wife, who gave him children
When he asked, who pressed his pants with perfect lines,
Who fed him what she had. Even now, no peace for her, him lying
At her side. He never appeared in my dreams, but
Lately he's been coming round, making visits,
Standing in front of me showing off his skills:
Molding mud and straw into perfect bricks of earth.
He stops to admire his work. His fingers caked with mud,
He opens his fly and pisses on his art. He stands grinning,
His urine drying in the sun. He sticks out his chin
So God can see his Tarahumaran face (a gift he stole from
The mother he forgot). I smell his hat, stained with
Sour sweat: he wore it always, loved it deeper than
His daughters—and with reason—they would not mold
To his head. I see his eyes, black, awful even now.
I see his thick stern lips, the hint of a smile he never
Wore in life. His skin is the color of the dirt that
Swallowed him long before he died. He was misnamed
Ventura, and now, twenty years after his death,
He has the balls to stand in front of me, still blind
Not speaking. He disappears when I begin to open my mouth

But he will come again. Uninvited, he will walk
Into my house some sunny day—and I will grab him
By the collar of his well-pressed khaki shirt:

"Your wife and all your children worked the fields
Of white, picking endless rows of cotton that was

Anything but soft. You claimed their money as yours—
Your thirst was greater than their hunger. You'd leave

Them broke. But when their money was gone, you
Reappeared yelling for water, clothes and food (no

Repentance in your shouts). In the house where you were
Lord, forgiveness was no virtue learned from priests

But a necessary rule for those who lived
With you. You appeared and disappeared several times

A year. Old man, you must have thought yourself
An excellent magician…." He would raise

His fist to stop me, "Chivo" on his lips. He would
Roll a cigarette, and flick it hard as if to say

I was nothing more than ash. His eyes would blaze
With rage for showing no respect—for him—my mother's

Father. But I would stand, not shrink from his accusing
Grin. No longer a boy, and every ounce his grandson,

I would swing my fist, and return him to his grave.

A year later, you're still nesting
In my head. Are you trying to find
A comfortable place to rest? Live
And breathe—through me? My body's
Not big enough for both of us to speak.

Old man, if you're trying to edge
Toward my heart, the best of luck
To you. Anger is a wall only the strongest
Can scale
                    But, I suppose,
That failing to reside in my heart,
You'll settle for an eloquent retraction.
That, I understand. After all, in death
All that's left on earth is reputation.

I'll tell you what, old man, I'm cold
But not yet frozen. You've lived in me
Long enough to loose another memory:

At seventy-seven, you were sick
and dying. I was seventeen.
You were brought to rest inside our house
on Calle Española. You were all but dead.
Considering your life, you looked
not bad.
                    Helpless as you were,
I was still afraid.
I always thought you'd hurt me.
You made a living cursing
the children of your children.
Had you been paid for that
you'd have retired
to a middle class existence.

My mother was sad when
She brought you home. One night
(it was spring), you were sleeping
in my parents' bed, and you beckoned
with your finger as I was walking
past that door. Trembling
I came close to you. Barely able
to speak, you whispered and pointed
at your penis and motioned—
you couldn't piss alone.
But seeing you in need
I ran away. I couldn't help
or touch you.

Once

in your life
you asked your grandson
for help—

he turned his back on you.

If you are not a hero
in this tale

then neither is your grandson.

IX.
A Final Prayer For Ventura

The smell of stale tobacco
Poured from your Indian skin. You needed
A bath, needed to be clean.

I'd never hug you dirty.
You drank and drank for hours
Sat and sat. The front of the shack
Where Teresa kept her stove—her place of work—
Your favorite place to loiter. Day after day
The only part of you that moved (No,
Not your brittle heart) was your
Thin and aging elbow
That moved that shiny beer can
Toward chapped and flaking lips.

❧

My mother never speaks about your life, but she
Reminds us all: *He used to sing. My God, he*
Used to sing. A dark and perfect angel. Old man,
If I had to sing for my food, I'd starve—sure
As shit I'd die hungry. But I have taught myself
To speak. Having been born to the realism
Of my dying century, I fight the urge to make
A romance of your life.

And yet I conjure you
A poet. I see you singing, guitar
In love with your hands. My mother is a girl,
Smiling at the god who sings to her. Teresa,

In the light, is watching you. She hums
And she is blessed to be your wife.
I want to light a candle in your memory.
I want to pay for masses for your soul.
                    I want to love   God
Damnit, man, why did you stop singing?

Prayers for the Holy and the Dead

*Unless a grain of wheat
falls to the earth and dies,
it remains alone;
but if it dies
it bears much fruit.*
    —JOHN 12:24

Growing Memories

The harvest is rich but the laborers are few.
                                        —LUKE 10:2

for Larry

                    You are growing corn
This year. You stick out your summer hands
Calloused and blistered from turning
The stubborn soil of your garden. You care
For it with quiet, with wonder as if you were
Nursing a child, and you remember: the boy ran
Among the rows as if the fields were forests
Planted for his games. The boy knew nothing
Of what the earth demanded. You remember.

                    You imagine the sweetness
That is to come. You can almost taste it. You speak of
The coming yellow, and the color in your speech
Hits the air like a brush sweeping the sky with
The growing season of Wisconsin summers preserved in the pores
Of your palms which you cannot wash clean. That yellow
Burns in your mouth. It is the taste of someone's hands
(German ancestors or some Indian farmer long dead);
The taste of someone's hands who, having survived
The white winter, planted inherited seeds
And fed them with the waters of his blood
Hoping the summer would resurrect his dead.

                    This year, there are scars
On your hands. The hurt in them has worn away
Your youth. You have formed yourself

Into a farmer who plants not for the future
But for the past. You are not growing corn.
You are growing memories.

Uncles (Who Lie Still and Perfect)

Guillermo

       I would fix my eyes on him. He looked right
past me. I was a ghost (as we all were in that slumbering

world of his). Sometimes he suspected I was there:
I wore white shirts, the only color he could see.

Having risen late from a bed he never shared, he sat
stiller than his chair. His waking moments were hard.

He sat solid, immutable, deflecting the light of a sun
that was a heavy burden. He lived for the night, and saw

darkness pasted to his eyes. No stars there, never any
stars. I think he never saw them. The dullness on his

face, a milky film, a veil. Not even the flame of his mother's
anger (nor her impatient love) could peel it from his

skin. At least he knew she was there (and why shouldn't
he know?—He lived with her). She scolded him as she

handed him a second bowl of soup: Ya basta de tanto trago.
Te estás matando. Y a mi también. Me estás matando. He nodded,

almost ashamed. And never answered. His marriage to the
bottle lasted twenty years, a union consummated every evening

of his youth. And only after that great divorce that left him
for the first time alone, did he take a wife. He became

a man in mourning, the veil never lifting from his face.
Many years he kept a cancer (something he brought home

from a bar one night—and locked it like a treasure
in his liver). It pounded him month after month, hit him

and hit him until he fell forever in his bed. No liquor
to soften the blows, he fought long as he could. Stranger

that he was, I keep his picture on an altar in my house.
I rise in the morning, his image so familiar I do not

even see it. Now, it is he who's the ghost.

Ricardo

The night
that man
took a brick
to your head
your mother slept.
But there was no
rest for her.
She tossed
and tossed
as she dreamed

she saw you, happy man
of her world. Your smile
more real   that moment
than her breath. You sat,
she saw you, happy man
a pebble in your hand, such
joy in simple holdings.
The sun surrounding you

in familiar embrace. She could
see your face, strong, her
peace in you. Your eyes,
the same color as the
cotton leaves of summers
gone, she watched them
close. Then nothing but
clouds. Some large shadow
came between you
and the sun. From where
she slept she cried
"Run!" You could not
see what she saw, could not
hear her voice. All you felt
was the brick
pound your skull.
When the letter arrived
she did not open it.
She had already read
the word that spelled
your death.

My whole life
all I have heard
of you
is that you were
beauty itself.
When your name
is spoken, it is
as if you were
in the room
listening.

Bernardo

"Cada cabeza es un mundo": the basis of his thought.
The first philosopher I met in the flesh—the only one
I can still quote verbatim. (So much Descartes and Hegel
In the shaping of my mind—and all their words forgotten.
It's true they were smart, true they earned their fame,
Revered and remembered and argued with respectfully—
But what is that to me? What I want to know is
What kind of uncles were they?)

                    There was something in his step
That made me think he could dance (though I never saw him
Gliding over ball rooms). His walk was dance enough.
The only uncle I ever imagined having sweet and sweaty
Sex with his wife of many years. I knew he held her tight
And whispered her name again and again until she was
Safe and asleep. He wasn't ashamed of his mind, of his
Heart, of his penis: the first anti-dualist, anti-oppositional
Thinker in six or seven generations. He never hid his body
From his soul, and at his peak, he argued down ten or twenty
Arm-chair gnostics per night at his favorite bar.

He carried himself like a flame daring the wind to
Blow him out. He never lost his passion for the bottle
Yet he never lost his mind. I yearned to have his fight,
The best of all the graces. *"Mira, mijo, somos*
Lo que somos": Impossible to live with, he died alone
But did not die unloved. My God, what a heart you had.
What a mind. You left no body of work, no written will,
Not a single letter. What a heart. What a waste.
I've had to settle for reading Plato and Augustine.

Benjamín

On the day of his birth
He took a breath, opened his eyes, then
Closed them tight forever. There was
Something in the Texas air he could never
Be at peace with—too much blood in the dust,
Too much fire in the sun, too much wind,
Too much wind. There would never be enough
Rain. He was born too thirsty. Knowing this
Though he was born perfect and good,
He died.

Many years passed before his
Surviving older brother (under instructions
From a mother who refused to forget)
Passed down his name to his son.

This is how I
Came to be possessed of his name, which
In turn, made me fall in love with dead
Uncles who lie still and perfect. Perfect
And good in the ground.

In Memory of my Uncles:
Guillermo Sáenz, Benjamín Sáenz,
Ricardo Alire, and Bernardo Alire

Fences

I was six.
The fence was high   and as I leapt
the barbs   wrote perfect lines
straight across   my chest.
My skin ripped easy   as a rag.

I dangled there
my blood was   thick and red.

That was when
I first began
to know the price
of jumping
over fences.

~

In love with women
and men, he says they're both
the same: "I could close
my eyes and groan and groan
all night. Hands are hands.
And when they knead
my body like bread
I rise to meet the touch."

~

Sad and old, she opened her house
to elders knocking at her door.
They promised to visit her
daily. She agreed to join

their church. She was asked
to rid herself of statues
saved on altars in her room.
She told them she was ready
to renounce. Next day, when they
returned, she told them how she'd
thrown her statues out: "I beat
them into nothing." Each day
when the elders left her home,
she took her statues from a closet
and raised them back to life.

≈

A drink in hand, she talks:
"When I have sex
my mind dissolves.
In the everything of touch,
the nothingness of language
disappears. When thought
returns, I am left with sadness
and with words. I want to live
on the silent side of speech."

≈

I stood before
the Torah. I searched
for Yahweh's name whose face
cannot be seen, whose name
cannot be said.
     When I found
letters that stood
for his name, I touched them

trembling. Lines on fragile
parchment: what about them
takes us close to God?

———

I write in English, dream
in Spanish, listen to Latin chants.
I like streets where
Chicanos make up words.
Sometimes, I shout
Italian words to wake
the morning light.
At dusk, I breathe out
fragments of Swahili.
I want to feel words
swimming in my throat
like fighting fish
that refuse to be hooked
on a line.

Clay Woman Holding Her Sacred Heart

To Karen (who already knows)

Nun? Saint? Penitent whore? Devoted follower of The Little Flower
Of Jesus or reincarnation of Hester Prynne? Other clay figures around her,
But they—they wear yellow and pink robes of spring, hold candles,
      flowers,
Children in their arms, hands closed tight around the treasures they adore.
Strong as they are, what they hold fast with their arms
      must someday be
Unloosed, but not today. She stands near those created by the same
Hands, the same clay, yet she lives separate. In her Lenten
      garments she stands
Solitary—in a strange exile. She is of the earth, nothing more than dirt,
But
                  She has been elected by her maker to be a beacon
In the night, to fight, to suffer with her devils and her God. She walks in
Darkness, walks in light—withstands the loneliness of life. She holds
Open her palms. She is holding a thing bigger than her hands—awful
And red as the winter sun sinking into a cold cold sea. It is a heart
She holds, the heaviest of burdens. The heart is wet with blood. She was
Molded, baked, painted in Mexico where any saint worth
      praying to must be
Adorned with blood as well as gold. Among the poor, blood's the proof
Of faith. One pays for holiness with flesh.
                In El Norte, we like our icons
Bloodless. We believe in woundless resurrections. We like
      our tombs empty
And well-swept. In the North—where we live—the poor
      have no advantage:

Blessed be the poor—and blessed be the rich for they are poor in spirit.
The Kingdom of God is lovely and conveniently democratic.
    Unless a grain
Of wheat falls to the earth and dies, it remains alone; but if it dies,
It bears much fruit. Let us not speak of the price. Let us not
Speak of the heart that must be ripped from its safe,
      protected place.
        She holds
This bloody heart as if it were the largest jewel on earth.
She exhibits her breakable stone, the place where sorrows begin—
Sorrows that have stained her hands and garb with indelible marks
Of pain. She cannot wash that source of torment in the world.
    She will not
Hide the visible sign that makes her use her hands—the sign that forces
Her to touch: hands steady, she holds out her only offering. Older now,
She has learned her own secrets. She has cast out the shame of her past.
She no longer has need of her pride. She is no longer afraid to surrender
Her last possession. It has been given many times. She has felt its
Absence, wept each time she has lost it: each time growing accustomed
To the lifelessness of losing it, each time embracing the numbness
Of nothingness. But always the heart returned beating strong as the wings
Of a young eagle in first flight.
      Look closely at her face. See,
She is not in mourning. Her days of weeping are behind. *This is her day*
Of freedom. Palms open, she offers her sacred heart....*Unless a grain*
Of wheat...   Sins, she has many, but she can't repent
From the giving. There is peace in public stigmata...*but if it dies,*

A hundred wheatfields for the poor,

    a million loaves of bread for those who want.

Arturo, Your Mother

and his mother kept all these
things in memory
                    —LUKE 2:51

for Jovita

          She sat on the edge
Of your bed, her mourning hands
Ironing out the creases in your sheets.
An endless task. (So many wrinkles,
Arturo, and she's still dreaming of smooth.
She was born to iron.)

         In grief, she searched the room. I
Disappeared and she saw you—in your room again—
She reached—   Her voice, quiet,
Quiet, listening to the fragments of your
Boyhood in the room: the unforgiving
Blade of your life cutting and cutting
And cutting. Your death everywhere
On her face, but what did I know
Of her wounds? What does a childless
Man—what—what does he know about sons and their
Deaths? About first words and final breaths?

          On the edge of your bed—the edge,
Too, of her life. How many more years—for her?
The air she breathes is nothing but memory and grief.
As she sat, she stared at your many colored coats;
She wrapped them in her arms:

"Today. Cremating him. Today.
He's ashes now."

She was bent in the wind of your death.
Her tears, a rain watering your house,
But they would never grow you back to life.
Never never grow you back to life.

My mother, too, has worn
That look, that hurt, has lost a son, lost him
To that straight and pretty angel that flicked you off
This earth as a lord would

flick an insect

off his plate.

I hate, I hate that messenger of death. His heavy hand
Is cruel to crooked sons, and cruel, too, to those that gave
Them life. You'd think my mother—and yours—would have
Grown accustomed to their losses. Raised to accept, accept,
Accept. They never cursed God and rebelled (Born to bear
But never break—is that what we decided? In the myths
Their sons create, they know love *and only love.* What if
They hate that angel more than any of their sons?)

The last time I was with you,
You sat up weak in a wrinkled bed, and caught
Each breath of air like a pigeon
Begs for crumbs: hungry for health, for words,
For anything tossed in your path. "I thought
Of your mom, was thinking and thinking of her."
Generous, you died, thinking of the living.

She gave me your coats.
I look fine in them, Arturo (that's of
Little comfort. You did not buy them for
Surviving friends). I asked her for your hat, the one
You bought and wore to protect you from the heat:
The medicine you took turned your skin to wax—
Without your hat you might have melted in the sun.
That day, when you returned to ash, your mother
Searched your closets and gave away your clothes.
In grief, she is giving life. She is pregnant
With the memory of her son. She will dress
And sleep in sorrow, and when she wakes
You'll be thumping, thumping, thumping in her heart.

Contemplating Roads

She said there were times when she was lost
But something pulled her through always
Just when she thought she would break: "What keeps
Us sane, I wonder, any of us? Is there a hand
That keeps our minds in place when others
Work to tear them out? Is there a hand?" Her man cracked
Her ribs so often she walked slow and bent,
"But it isn't all his fault. As long as I can
Remember I've walked as if I was carrying a heavy
Sack of dirt." She almost died from loving him. "Leave
That bastard, leave," I used to urge. But she
Would shut me up. "It's up to me to call
Him names." She'd point to one of her bruises as if
They were there from birth. "I've earned the right
To call him anything I please—including lover."
And then she'd look at me. OK, OK, I'd nod
"But you should leave him." She took my advice
More than once but she always went back, the only
Path she knew: "That road's been worn by me alone.
I know it, walk it every day. You want me to marry
Some tight-ass gringo who treats his woman
Equal but leaves his conscience in his yard?
The men who run the maquilas, they don't
Hit their wives. But those women in their sweatshops—
What are they to them? I wouldn't give you
A deflated peso for a man who wears a tie. You know
Why they wear them?" She laughs, "To cut off
Their hearts from their minds. The man I love is not

The best there is—but he is not the worst.
He only hurts his wife."

       After his death, her eyes grew younger,
The blows of his ghost landing lighter on her body.
His shadow is everywhere on her face, her
Hands, her tired walk. All that time
She was with him I thought she was sick, all
Her mistakes as clear as water in a glass. Her
Bruises and scars a public exhibit of woman
Trapped by man.   But
I know nothing of her tears, know nothing of her love
That keeps her sane in that important kind of way
Some people have after they've lost everything,
No longer afraid of who might take what
They have, what they own, what they've paid for.
That kind of sanity gives everything away
Before it's ever taken.
             She's done
With men, but still likes to look at their eyes,
Their swaying bodies as they walk. "But I aint
Buying nothing that comes from their tongues.
Mejor sola que mal acompañada."

She gives me coffee and talk. She drinks
Her coffee black swishing the bitterness around
In her mouth. "Ummm. I love this stuff. You can
Taste the hands that picked it. I never did learn
To drink anything with sugar." Her voice rises,
The first star of twilight, then falls again

To earth. "How come we let this country
Beat us senseless? Everywhere, we're falling,
Knocked down as we walk. But it isn't true
That we're lost, that we've been stopped dead
In our tracks." She brushes back her hair that often
Hides her face. "In America roads mean much, roads
Connect everything, everyone, black roads, hard,
The veins of a nation. Roads, they weren't made
For us. Nor we for them. And *my road,*
I'll pound and pound, and pave it as I walk."

Hermanos

Am I my brother's keeper?
            —GENESIS 4:9

                    At school, they held
him back a year, put him in a class with those
who did not take to books. His English
was loose; he was never in love with someone else's
grammar. We were in the same grade, he and I, but
I was in another class—with boys and girls who talked
correct and white, and raised their hands. I never
fought—not then. I learned to act like them, spoke
English like a native. I was more at home in their
world than my brother who was darker, my brother
who was alien in the country of words and pens
and paper. Unbrothered in that public place
of learning and unlearning. *I thought you hated me*
for being good at school. Was it me who hated you?
Was I ashamed?
                    I ached to hit home runs,
but never made the team. My brother wore a cap,
and had a number of his own. School was mine, but
come the summer, all the world was his. *I never yelled*
"Go! Go!" I never yelled, "That's my brother! That's
my brother!" as you scored a run or caught a fly.
I went to every game.

Together, we learned to swim in dirty ditches;
together we fed the hogs and chickens on our farm;

together we learned to hoe in the hot sun
hating the hard labor. We were taught to pray to
the same God, light candles in front of the same
saints. We were both named after dead uncles we
never knew, never loved   *When you saw*
the clouds of summer, did you see virgins and saints?
When you heard the rain, did you hear God?
Ricardo, in our teens, did we ever ever speak?
You never told me what you thought. I never asked.
I was not your friend. I graduated, went to college,
became addicted to books. You never finished
high school, joined the Army, became addicted
to drugs. You were in that place to heal yourself.
Your hair was short—they'd shaved your head—like
Uncle Willie used to cut our hair. For a week,
They let you out. You stayed with me. I didn't
know if you were sad or hurt. Is it hard?—
I wanted—I wanted to ask—to yell: "You can
do it. You can do it. Heroin is strong
but, Ricardo, you are stronger." We went
to movies, ate burgers, tacos, pizza. You ate
and ate. Ricardo, you were hungry.

My father's brother is dying. Soon he will
take his place in the camp of permanent exile,
unreachable. The biggest piece of him that will
survive is the part of him lodged in my father's
memory. An undirected anger flares in his eyes
as he speaks *of him,* his brother, who was never
his best friend.

"Qúe milagro's" how you greet me
when you call me on the phone. I'm never home,
you say, but always call. You tell me you quit
smoking, and say you're gaining weight.
"Me, too," I laugh. Me, too.

My father's
brother is dead: as he stares into the past,
it becomes solid and sad. He pulls out
the sharp slivers of his brother. He holds
the pieces tight in his fists, trying to keep
from bleeding, fighting to hold the fragments
that spell his brother's name. But the pieces
are tired and brittle, turning to dust in his fist
even as they cut. Nothing can stop the hurting.

Ricardo, the last time I entered
your house, I stared at the lunch pail you'd molded
with your hands. You welded it, designed,
created it. You buffed and buffed
until it wore a halo. In the surface of your work
I saw the sun, my self, the past. I saw us
running through the rows of autumn cotton,
everything soft and white and warm. Ricardo,
Stay.
Stay forever in this world.

To John (When He Was Five)

You opened my door at dawn. You
Dove into my bed. You breathed
Into my face. The breeze from your
Young mouth smelled like an orchard
Of peaches. "Wake up!" you cried,
"Wake up!" Your voice, small as your
Hands exploring my eyes, my hair,
My unshaved face. "Wake up!" you laughed
Then ran away. For you, it was a game.
Your uncle was a playmate. You left
Me there, the sour taste of morning
In my mouth. Peaches, John, peaches.
They are all you know, all you have tasted.

Come back. You woke me, come and stay.

On Observing the Pigeons
at Union Square (San Francisco)
On the Eve of the Gulf War.

The stone is gray as January's sky.
This column is a monument to dark
pigeons. *Erected by the citizens of San Francisco*
To commemorate Poseidon stands atop
the granite column. His triton poised
the victory of the American Navy
under Commodore Dewey at Manila Bay,
May 1st, 1898. Pigeons beg and eat
and shit. *An uncle served in Korea—*
I remember—when he was shipped
to fight, I listened to men whispering
war They have made this their home.
Protected in the shade of this monument;
these birds will praise it till they die.
I would stare at his picture, handsome,
in a uniform. I would repeat: Ko-re-a,
Ko-re-a. This is not a bird that knows
a song: it cannot sing of sorrows, cannot
praise. *My brothers grew, put on suits*
of soldiers like those that came before.
They circle and land, circle and land.
No flying south in winter, no
flying north in spring. Every season
in their feathers is the same. *Look, they*
circle again. Basest of all the birds, there is
no God or freedom in their flight.

The Adoration of the Infant Jesus

Nostalgia, from
nostos: a return home; and
algos: to be in pain

After Mass this Christmas Day
The people file out. This is
All? Where are the lines?
Expectant crowds? The clamoring
Children waiting to kiss His feet?

I am standing with my mother, my father, my brothers,
And my sisters. I am standing on the tips of my toes
Stretching to see above the heads of those in front.
We crowd into the aisles, shove and push. I smell
Work and perfume; I smell starch and a woman's iron
On the immaculate clothes of those who stand and wait.
We stand together. Here, I am safe—protected in the warmth
Of Spanish. God is so in love with us. I can't wait
To see him. To kiss him, to kiss him. When my lips reach
His feet, he will turn to flesh. I know this. He will
Turn softer than silk, warm as a summer's night,
And he will smile at me. When I reach the holy place,
I stare at the priest who holds the Savior in his arms,
The altar boy who wipes His feet after every kiss.
The priest nods, and when my lips touch the child I have
Waited for, he is warm with the kisses of the people.

I feel the pulse of his blood running through the softness
Of his feet. I know he is breathing. He is alive. He
Is ours. The priest does not know what he holds,
But we who have kissed him, know that he is real.

The people here
Do not believe
In lines. Some of us
Do not walk out
The doors. We cannot
Leave this church.
We are few, but we are
Sober as the morning winter
Light. Slowly, one by one,
We kneel before the scene:
A mother, a father, a son;
The sheep, and kings, an angel.
We have known them all our lives.
Mary, the Virgin, the Mother;
Joseph, the Worker, the Father.
The child, the Lover of flesh.
We will love them all our lives.

for Rose

To the Desert

I came to you one rainless August night.
You taught me how to live without the rain.
You are thirst and thirst is all I know.
You are sand, wind, sun, and burning sky,
The hottest blue. You blow a breeze and brand
Your breath into my mouth. You reach—then *bend*
Your force, to break, blow, burn, and make me new.
You wrap your name tight around my ribs
And keep me warm. I was born for you.
Above, below, by you, by you surrounded.
I wake to you at dawn. Never break your
Knot. Reach, rise, blow, *Sálvame, mi dios,*
Trágame, mi tierra. Salva, traga, Break me,
I am bread. I will be the water for your thirst.

Through the Rooms of This House

You play. Slowly, your fingers, your touches
Rot the strings. You must replace them. Nothing lasts
Not the white of boyhood snow, not the house
You loved when you were five, not the earth-raw beets
You bit when you were eight. You know this. It is
Why your fingers are calloused. It is why you play.

At dawn, at dusk, at night
You pick up your guitar, place it on your lap
And touch the wood, the tamed and tender
Strings you bend and release. Bend and release.
Your hands begin to sweat. Years of wearing your habit,
Years of suffering your hands, after years
Of being held in the practice that longs for
Perfect, your guitar now smells of you. Your fingers
Are part of the wood, part of the grain, part of the sounds
That rush through the rooms of this house. The notes
Float from the place where your fingers scar
The strings, cannot be held or kept, vanish

Only to return when you have left the room.

Prayer

for George

>   The sky
> is clear as gin.
> I could lay my body
> down, sleep in the calm
> night, the peace of the winter
> wind, and the deep black
> sky that makes me forget
> the morning light. Makes me
> remember. Now I see
> the stars, a million tongues
> of fire. I am so
> small. The earth beneath
> my feet is giving, strong,
> but slowly slowly
> dying. Tonight
> I want

> *there has to be a God*

Summer

~

*He will wipe away every tear from their
eyes and death will be no more, neither shall
there be mourning nor crying nor pain any
more, for the former things have passed away.
....Behold I make all things new.*
—Revelations 21:4–5

The Wedding Feast at Cana

This, the first of his miracles, Jesus
performed at Cana in Galilee, and manifested his glory.
                                          —John 2:11

for Larry and Katy

A man and woman meet. They fall
in love. This has been written; this
has been read; this is an old story.

In the body   there is a place:
those who work will know this space,
will know it's hard and holy, will
know it wears away the heart. We may
curse it day and night; we may
speak of it, point to it, pray to it—
it will not be appeased.

        Listen to your names:
their sounds are like
no other: whispers of the world
needing to know if there is joy.
Is there joy? Listen to the hunger
forever—that song will never cease.
The song is sad. *You*
will never be full. Stay. Listen
to the hunger. Do not turn
from that sound. You cannot
run from earth. *Naked*

*you came from the dirt. Naked you must
return.* Flesh is flesh and it is flesh
till death.

                     This day, words
like thirst, and flesh, and hunger
mean *marriage.* Water is turned
into wine. This is the day of miracles.
Take. Drink. The best has been
saved for the poor. Taste. This is the cup
of salvation. Be drunk. Touch. Make love
through the lonely night—but when you wake
remember: this wine is good and sweet
but you will thirst again.

The book of life is hard to write:
it is written with bone and blood;
it is written with hearts that labor
and labor, beat and beat until the walls
fall down. Begin. Write: in the kingdom
of the naked, working heart
shame is banished. A man and woman
meet—this is an old—*write it!*
Begin. Begin. Begin.

Gloria. Woman Becoming Her Name.

Five years old, she stuck
Her hand through a wringer: her bones
Refused to break. She learned to cuss,
She learned to fight, that girl refused
To bend. She stole her mother's make-up,
Sometimes stole the car. Still a girl,
She wore a bra, wore the body
Of a woman twice her age.

                            She never
Loved soft men—liked them hard as stone.
She scratched her name on them: they
Remembered who she was. At eighteen
She was married. He loved the bottle
More than he loved her. She lived
Poor, took nothing with her
When she left—except her little girl.

        A daughter on her lap, she was
A rocking chair. She swung her baby
Down, lowered her near the ground, then
Gently pulled her back, raising her forward
And up—towards her waiting lips. When
Their game was done, her daughter pressed
So close that they were one:
a blossom from a cactus in the Spring.

        She met a man
Who had no need to rule. On the day

She married him, the winter sun reflected
Off her face. More children and a man.
She worked hard, and she was loved—

LAS CRUCES—Saturday morning two men walked into the bowling alley
at 1201 E. Amador Ave. shortly after 8 a.m. Once inside the killers herded
seven people into the office, made them lay down and shot them in the
backs of their heads. Stephanie Senac and her daughter Melissa, 12, were
among the survivors. Steve Teran, 26, his stepdaughter Paula Holguin 6,
and Valerie, 2, were also inside the bowling alley. They died as a result of
their gunshot wounds. Also inside was Amy Houser, 13. She was found
dead at the scene.

Five years, and grief's reshaped her life.
Daughters die, but do not die. The empty womb
Remembers. Sorrow molds the hours of her
Days; sorrow molds her flesh. She carries
In her voice the silence she has known. She has
Dug into her stillness, and in the coldness

Of that desert,
          she has found her name.

Altars Into Time

An alien people clutching....Ad altare dei

New Mexico, 1959

The sun forgave in May. The spring winds
Dead. Crops, new and garden green, rising in
The fields. In June, the sun would belt: a harsh
Father beating useless sons. In June, the sun
Would not forgive, every one guilty before
The hanging judge. For now, the summer was
Far enough away. Today, a festival of prayer.
Here, no one knows the May pole, no parades
Of workers clamoring for rights—contracts, unions,
Strikes as alien as rain. No city streets. Here,
Roads are paved with dust. Old adobe homes
And hungry dogs and outhouses—a place ignored
By gringo time....

Altars in Time I

Josefina made an altar out of a wood dresser where she kept her
favorite saints. She worshiped San José on summer afternoons. I didn't
know what her novenas meant—I was in love with leaning into her, with
the sound of her voice, the feel of her soft cotton dress against my face as
she prayed. She smelled of work and lilac. Teresa had statues everywhere
in her house. I have a picture of her standing before the saints that she
kept on her fireplace. Everything in her house was an altar. The altar at
San Albino's in Mesilla is stuck in my memory like a nail that cannot be
pulled from the wall—when I am in pain I think of it. When I was a boy,
watching the priest stand behind the altar wearing his heavy robes made

me feel holy. My mother keeps an altar in her bedroom. She has a big statue of the Immaculate Heart of Mary. She and my dad keep a candle lit in one of the bedrooms: it's a prayer for their children. When I made my first communion I was surprised that God tasted like cardboard. The taste did not matter: this was Jesus. At St. Thomas seminary, the altar was simple. It, too, was made of wood. I read the scriptures. I studied theology. I learned words: christology, transubstantiation, eschatology, exegesis, hermeneutics. I read Augustine and Aquinas, *the confessions, the proofs for the existence of God.* When I became a priest, I stood behind the altar and lifted the host toward heaven every day. I've never stopped loving the Mass, but the robes were heavy for my body. One day, no longer able to walk, I took them off. Many years later, I had a heavy dream. Chimayo was calling. I woke and built in altar in my house. I made it out of wood, and burdened it with faces that I love.

New Mexico, 1959

Today, in this town
Filled with more drinkers than saints, a crowd
Gathers round the altar of the Virgin to pray
Saint Dominic's beads. (Had he imagined us here? Had
Dominic dreamed this future?) The statue, dressed
In satin and blue, is crowned with early yellow roses
Grown in my grandmother's garden. She leads the singing,
Knows the Catholic hymns better than she's ever
Known her husband. Her old voice quivers
Like a dandelion's cotton in the breeze. The women
Follow her voice   half a step behind. The songs
Are old and brittle like the pages of novenas
Whose words are worn with use. The clatter
Of the beads rings out like wooden chimes

Calling us to kneel. The decades, ten Hail Mary's,
One Our Father, ten Hail Mary's, one Our Father,
Last forever to a boy, but the look on Mama's face—
Who could see me through shut eyes—tells me,
I, too, will still myself and pray. I never could
Rebel against her face. When I was five, she ruled
The world. Virgins, saints and angels—even God—
Were nothing in her presence.

Altars in Time II

The Aztecs had altars of sacrifice   How many women knelt at
the altar of Athena? How many prayers did she answer?   My
mother once went on a pilgrimage to the Cathedral of
        Our Lady of Guadalupe in Mexico City.
Eat, eat, thou hast bread; Drink, drink, thou hast water
Abel offered the good fruits of his labor on an altar to God, and
God was pleased
All the steam in the world could not, like the Virgin, build Chartres
I once went to Mass at the tomb of St. Peter's beneath the main
altar of the basilica
        Do this in memory
        At Lourdes, wooden crutches hang over the grotto
        Heart of Sky, Heart of Earth
        give us our sign, our word,
        as long as there is day, as long as there is light.
        When it comes to the sowing, the dawning,
        will it be a greening road, a greening path?
        Give us a steady light, a level place   and we will
build you an altar   In Juárez, in the chapel next to the
Cathedral, the old people place milagros at the feet of

statues.　　　Return our hearts　　　Men who've pulled themselves up by their own bootstraps should remember the workers who've crafted their boots　　　Abraham built an altar in the desert　*I refuse to accept the idea that man is mere flotsam and jetsam in the river of life which surrounds him. I refuse to accept the view that mankind is so tragically bound to the starless midnight of racism and war that the bright daybreak of peace and brotherhood can never become a reality*

I watched a very old man today who was still strong enough to pick up his grandson and toss him in the air.

Patricia! Larry! Karen! Linda! Did I tell you? Gloria, Norman, Amy! Ricardo! Mom! Dad!—Did I tell you? Did I tell you all? I dreamed we built an altar—

New Mexico, 1959

Every evening in May, we knelt, and after we had
Prayed, we stood repeating litanies, chants, and songs
That brought out all the stars. (They shone
Like silver crosses in the sun.) I could see
By light of candles, a nearness to tears in the eyes
Of all the women. But the Virgin seemed unmoved.
Perhaps she did not hear us. This unschooled Spanish:
Sad, strange, unknown to her.

　　　　　　　　　Each passing day, the sun grew hot,
Then hotter. Until at last, the sweat streamed out of us
Faster than our prayers. On the final day of May
Our offerings to the Queen of Heaven ended.
The women, flowered like their gardens,
Brought out food enough to fill our stomachs
Twice. Empanadas, pasteles, for us and our cousins,

Piñatas, punch with lemons and limes. At last,
Free to dive in the dirt and rub away the prayers
That had left us stiff and clean.
                            The food devoured,
The singing done, the women stripped the Virgin of her clothes—
And took away her altar. An empty platform in the center
Of the yard, and trash around it. Gone the singing, gone
The women, gone the whispered prayers. Gone the altars
Of May. Tomorrow, the work of cleaning, of tending
The weeded fields. Tomorrow: June. Our praying would not
Save us from the heat that was to come. That heat was hell.

Traveling to Chimayo

Chimayo. I traveled there—
Was summer—with a friend,
Stranger to that place, but
Living close to earth—
He knew—Pilgrims never walk
Alone—It was sacred—
Chimayo—he said the word—

In the sanctuary	Of the church
At Chimayo	There is a pit of dirt.
A legend	Has been handed down,
Generation	To generation,
That the dirt	Of Chimayo
Has the power	To heal.
Chimayo	I've heard
Your name	I've seen
Your pilgrims	Kneel

And heard
I did not
To theirs
I am ashamed
Not pray
I know
Returning

Them pray
Join my voice
At Chimayo.
I did
At Chimayo.
I will always be
To Chimayo.

I saw a father
Rub the miracle dirt
On the thin legs
Of his son.
The father said the hands
Of God were living
In the earth.

A long time, I have been
Traveling to Chimayo.
I have heard voices
Tossing words at God
Since that rainless day
At dawn when my
Grandmother's stubborn hands
Pulled me from the womb.

I once anointed a man
With the oils of the dying.
He was young, who lived
Reckless in a barrio
Who took a gun, played a game

With his friends as if it were
A toy. A white bandage
Held his brains intact.
His heart was pounding hard—
It filled the room.
Who has heard it
Can't forget the sound:
The heart's a fist that fights.
The heart is hard to kill.
I sometimes wake and see
The oils of the church
Glistening on his skin.

I once watched a child
Take her first breath
In the world. The child
Was once her mother, and then
The baby crossed a border.
When her cries hit the air
And she breathed, I knew
That sound:
Solid as the wood
Of any altar.

I have been traveling towards
These sounds all my life.
I have been traveling
Traveling toward the earth.

New Mexico, 1992

We learned to make the sign
                              of the cross,
Dipping earth stained hands in Catholic

Waters. We've filled the desert
                              with our altars.
We prayed our rosaries, played them,

Rubbed them, clutched them—
                              rattles in the wind
Swaying back and forth—our

Playground swings, we rode them
                              toward God,
Now hang them on walls or rear view

Mirrors of fixed-up '57 trucks.
                              Comenzamos
el Padre Nuestro en español but we

finish the prayer in a North
                              American tongue.
De vez en cuando we gather

ourselves together to baptize
                              a child
in the name of the Father, the Son,

and our ancestors who command us
                              from the grave.
We have made our way in the world,

worked hard, worked hard. Now, we
                                toss money
at the feet of my parent's grandchildren

like pilgrims tossed palms
                        before Christ.
In the sounds of our coins against

the concrete, I hear novenas
                        yellowing into dust.
We try to speak of our lives

purely. Our memories will not
                        let us.
We wear our culture as penitents

wear ashes on their foreheads,
                        Una mancha
permanente. We wake in strange-streeted

cities with the taste of the desert
                        in our mouths.
Because we are hungry, the taste

is sweet. We are damned to live
                        forever
on a border. From here, we build

our altars to our gods.

Between Worlds

The players dance on the field. The ball, as white
As a full moon in the clearest night of summer,
Bullets up, noiseless as it flies. Then falls.
It is not yet dark, but no longer day. The sun begins
To falter. Yet, in this momentary light, the grass is
Burning green, haloed, luminous. The shadows
Of men ceaselessly running, reach, touch me
And then again they run. They breathe hard, each intake
Of breath, a serious matter. They yell directions
To teammates in Spanish: *"¡Ahora sí!"* one yells
Then flips as he kicks the ball through the goal.
He lands on his feet laughing, his teeth whiter
Than the moon. He raises his arms in the air
As if to absorb the rays of a dying sun
And trap them in himself (he will save them in his
Body to light his moments of darkness). A companion
Runs to him, jumps in his arms, yells, *"¡Así, México, así!"*
And after the celebration, the play resumes.

Once in a playground
At school, two boys I knew were pulled from our team.
The best players, they could only watch for a week.
Their rough Spanish, an offense. "Foul ball. Play
In English." Like them, I spoke Spanish in my home,
Copied words in English on my page. Quick I learned
And soon my father's accent disappeared. English
Was mine, the language of my thought. But
Even now, the Mexico I never knew visits when I dream.
The top layer of memory's palimpsest washes clean

And what is left are prayers learned in tongues
Never to be banished.

                    A dark man
Whom someone called *"Bolivia"* juggles a ball
With a tap dance down the field. Like a ghost, a man
Appears, and takes the ball away. *"¡Perú!"* they yell,
"¡Perú!" He kicks the ball, effortless aim, to another,
And yells, *"¡Llevátela, Chile!"* They call each other
By native lands. They have come form another America
Distant, but here, tonight, the green grass
Is more theirs than those who planted it.

                    In El Paso
Caught between two countries, I played soccer on
Sunday afternoons with men who sought asylum,
Who lived crowded in homes for the poor, restless
With nothing but time for remembering. They fled
The newspaper cities of El Salvador, Guatemala,
Nicaragua, came to live and be at peace. I grew close
To one who came from there: he used to raise his arms
To shield himself when he heard familiar blades
Of helicopters. He would not speak of memories
That covered his face with the whiteness of a
Funeral pall. In those moments, though he remained
Beside me, his heart stole him away and I could not
Cross into his sacred awful country. And then
He would return.
                    He said strange things
About this country he adopted (but which never adopted
Him): "Such a rich country, and such bad streets. What

Do you do with your money?" He never understood
This America, was permanently lost. Troubled, he had
No place to go, picked up the ways of the streets, never
Spoke the truth about himself, was difficult to
Trust. He had scars, within and without, and his
Moods were dark as his eyes. He grew angry
When he drank, but I was not afraid. He
Was too hurt to hurt me.

                                        At my back
A crowd is gathered. They sit on blankets, feast
On healthy foods: salads and grapes, cheese and bread.
There is a quiet joy, expectant laughter, the waiting
For Shakespeare to come alive again. Tonight
A Midsummer Night's Dream (no better setting than a
Sky soon to be burning with stars). The actors
Will adopt Elizabethan speech. The words, having crossed
Oceans of time, will enter our hearts through accents
Distinctly "American." This will seem to no one out of place.
Our minds will open for the players. We will
Take them in. Theseus and Puck will weave their spells
Upon us. Love will cross and uncross, and all will be
Well in the end. The ball flies out of bounds. It almost
Strikes my face. But quick it is gone, on the field again.
The play that will soon begin behind me, as familiar
As the play before my eyes. Neither play is mine
Yet both beckon, call me from their separate worlds,
Will never let me go. Reluctantly, I turn. The Duke
Begins his speech:
        Now, fair Hippolyta, our nuptial hour
        Draws apace. Four happy days bring in....

The players in the distant field shout on, run on
Their game continues. Their muted Spanish shouts
Mix with careful iambics. The cacophony disturbs
A man behind me:

"Their games should cease. We've come to watch a play."

But soon enough
Too dark to run. The light shines only on the actors.
On the field, quiet. In peace, the play continues:
As the actors word their perfect lines, I see
Latin men in shorts taking perfect leaps
On perfect blades of grass.

In New Mexico, one summer,
I stood on Anazasi ruins. That day, the sky was so
Deep and so blue I felt I was, at last, out of
This tired century. As I touched a crumbling adobe
It was as if I had dipped my hand in waters of the
Church. This place: more full of God than any chapel
I had ever entered. This place: kinder than the cities
Of the world. I sat in caves the ancient ones
Had dug, the walls covered with the film of their
Smoke. But there were no bones here, no broken
Bodies or blood. Some angel or god had rolled back
The stone. These tombs were empty, everywhere
Voices: "I have lived. I have lived.
I am living."

From the opening in the stone
I could see an unpolluted earth, a canyon, more ruins

Near the stream. The sun lit them like candles. The waters
Of the stream: a hand that healed. And everything
Was green, though the air was dryer than the sand.
This was a desert. But this was not a desert. This was
A land that existed between times, between worlds, between
Water and drought. This was an ecotone, a place where
All borders were banished. Ruins from a disappeared
People, tourists with fluorescent T-shirts; desert snakes and
Rats made their nests under flowering shrubs; flies
And insects that flourished only in forests landed on vines
And cacti. There were sterile sands, and there was
Topsoil, dark and rich, where rows of corn had once
Fed hungry farmers. A cholla grew tall
Raising its thousand thorns to the Indian god of light,
And next to it, a ponderosa pine forever shed its
Needles. No voices yelled demanding: "Do not cross
This line that I have drawn." And no one asked,
"Why have you come? Who has brought you here?"
The wind, for reasons of its own, was pleased
To blow these seeds from other places and
Drop them in the soil. It pleased the rain
To make the seedlings grow.

Miracle in the Garden

"I have seen the Lord."
          —JOHN 20:18

You gave and gave, but it was not enough.
And there you were again—alone.
Another loss. Another wound. Another
scar: on the skin, in the heart, on the face.
The body wears the pain. Those hurts
come back—again—those hurts—again—
childhood and old lovers come back
always: they rise like Lazarus
needing no Jesus to command them back
to life. Overcome with grief—
more tears? So many droughts
and still more water in the well?
I sat across from you—in your garden—Spring—
and the sun shining like a new flower in bloom
haloing   you   me   the entire garden. You
did not notice the warmth. I was silent
in the presence of your grief. I was
there to pay respects, but not to speak.
In the sunlight, as I watched,
I had the urge to dip my hand
in the water of your tears,
and pray and bless myself
in the name of all your pain.

For a time, you walked that bridge
between the present and the past, between

this world and the next—*would it be better there?*
Your eyes stared blank—far—you
wanted to go, no longer wanting to choose
life. You sobbed out your regrets,
shook and shook your head. You clenched
your jaw as if to say: *I'll never love again,*
I'll never love. You grew quiet
listening to your god, or to your heart,
or to the western sun lighting up
the earth—the sun that set and rose,
the ceaseless sun that never tired
of the job that it was given. You felt
its labor on your skin. You were warmed—and then you
laughed. I saw you rising then. I saw you rise.

No sabe el río que se llama río

for Teresa

River, I've returned. This is where I learned
To love your waters—memorized the words, "drowning," "death,"
And "life." This is where I learned that I was flesh. *Fast
And hard, swim fast and hard. The race is for the swift.*
River, I remember summer afternoons. Those days were hot
And you were cool. I was softer then. Those summer waters
Gone now to the gulf, farther, farther, they have flowed
Toward greater waters—become a part of oceans vaster
Than the deserts of the earth. Waters flow into waters. My flesh
Began as water, grown hard as bone. I am *Individual.* In my
Tongue, that word is harsh and holy. And yet the peoples
Of the earth call: "Come." I want to flow into others, into
Bodies (there are no hearts without them), into that child
Who is touching a leaf for the first time in awe of the green,
Into that woman who fears the man she loves—I want to know
Her hunger. I want to flow into that dying man who's
Suffered years of hate because he would not walk the path
Of other men—that tired, hated man who daily wakes to offer
Silent thanks for the breath he steals each morning from
The dirty, stingy air; flow, flow into the scared and breathless
Man who runs across the desert, runs across the border,
Runs across the freeway, running, running, flow into his
Calloused hands—know and be his work. Know and be
His hands. I have spent my life shouting out my name:
I have spelled it out one letter at a time, and then stared hard

At what I was until I fell exhausted. I am tired of my name.
I am crooked from this yoke: from the heavy borders of "I am."

        We divide time into years. We divide
Years into seasons. We have different names for every river,
A different name for every ocean on the earth. But the
River does not know that we have named it "river"—it does
Not know that it is separate from the waters that call
"Come." Come. The river has flowed a thousand years. It is
Spring, and the river is spilling with the newness of winter's
Melted snow, each season flowing into each season. River,
I have been gone a long time. I am returning to your waters.
River, I've come back. River, I'm afraid. Carry me like water.

Meditation: Summer

A leaf floats
        down.

Bright yellow sliver
of tired tree.

The branch that once embraced
at last lets go
        of what it birthed in spring.

The leaf lands weightless

on the still-green grass.

There was no
greatness this summer,
caught in work, a squirming
fish on a hook.
To stay alive and fight
was all there was.
Every June, I tell myself:
this summer will be

a summer.
A real summer

like summers used to be:

Playing with friends,
learning to kiss,
swimming in ditches,
dancing on streets,
listening to afternoon rains.
Being a watcher of skies,
I knew about clouds,
about winds that washed
the earth. I knew
songs by heart,
used to write them down,
sing them, sing them
to myself, and then
to others. I spent
the summer listening
to the radio and the rain.
It was music
everywhere music.

I've ceased
to give thanks,
no longer attend
the sacrifice
of the Mass,
have lost
the power
to pray.
I've forgotten
the word, today.

Look! The tree

lets go

another leaf.

Octobers here are warm,
but it is October.
And the tree knows

it slowly

lets go

its summer.
There is no sadness for the tree.

It has lived its summer
in joy,

will spend the winter
in grief.

Spring will bring leaves
and alleluias.

This winter,
I am going to grieve.
I am going to wake
to every hurt
I've ever known—
every loss
I've left unturned

and plant seeds
in the cold fields
beneath those
heavy stones.
I let go all
my losses
before knowing
what they were
and why they were—
I let them go
before I ever
loved them.
I am going to spend
the season
paying them
my respects.
I am going
to robe myself
in mourning.
I will wipe my tears
with the burned ashes
of the garbs I wore
as a priest. *I am
dust.* I will beat
my breast
sanctus, sanctus, sanctus
like a drum
and know its music
sanctus, sanctus, sanctus.
I am dust.

I will listen to my
heart as it breaks,
kneel down and wail
like a wolf forced
to chew off his leg
to free himself
from the trap.
And to dust
I must return.
In the spring
I am going
to put away
my robes of mourning
and make myself
a white shirt.
It's damn time
I learned to sew
and let
the woman in me
breathe. Live.
After the season
of hunger and death,
I am going
to make a pilgrimage
to the tomb,
roll back the stone,
and race back home
full of all
the emptiness
I find there.

I will kill the fatted calf,
and gather those I've loved
from the highways
and byways I've walked.
I will take them
by their worn hands,
bathe them
and clothe them,
and ask them to
tell me of their labors,
of their lives,
of the difficult clays
that brought them forth.
Their speech will pound out
a new road. I will listen
and know why they were
born. I will listen
to the sweetness
of their words: I will put
them in a cup and drink them,
drink them down. A tree in summer
drinks the rain.
I will
to be that tree.

Benjamin Alire Sáenz

was born in 1954 in Old Picacho, a small farming village outside of Las Cruces, New Mexico, forty-two miles north of the U.S./Mexico Border. He was the fourth of seven children and was brought up in a traditional Mexican-American Catholic family. His family spoke mostly Spanish at home, and it was only through his education in the public schools that he learned to speak and write in English. He entered the seminary in 1972, a decision that was as much political as it was religious—he was heavily influenced by such Catholic thinkers as Thomas Merton, Dorothy Day, César Chavez and the Berrigan brothers. After concluding his theological studies at the University of Louvain, he was ordained a Catholic priest. Three and a half years later, he left the priesthood. At the age of 30, he entered the Creative Writing Program at the University of Texas at El Paso. He later received a fellowship at the University of Iowa, and in 1988, he received a Wallace E. Stegner Fellowship in poetry from Stanford University. In 1993 he returned to the border to teach in the Bilingual MFA program at the University of Texas at El Paso. The following year he married Patricia Macías, a woman he has known since high school.

Sáenz is the author of a previous book of poetry, *Calendar of Dust* (Broken Moon, 1991) which won an American Book Award. He is also the author of a collection of short stories, *Flowers for the Broken* (Broken Moon, 1992) and a novel, *Carry Me Like Water* (Hyperion, 1995).

This book is funded in part
by generous support from
the National Endowment for the Arts.

Book design, cover design and typography
by Vicki Trego Hill of El Paso, Texas.

The type is set in
Adobe Garamond and Runic Condensed.

Many thanks to Jim Ward
and Western Breed Records.

Printed on acid free paper
by Thomson Shore, Inc. of Dexter, Michigan.

∞

EL PASO • TEXAS